It's Time to Wine Down!

The Best 40 Wine Cocktail Recipes - Reds, Whites, Roses and Sparkles

BY

Daniel Humphreys

License Notes

No part of this Book can be reproduced in any form or by any means including print, electronic, scanning or photocopying unless prior permission is granted by the author.

All ideas, suggestions and guidelines mentioned here are written for informative purposes. While the author has taken every possible step to ensure accuracy, all readers are advised to follow information at their own risk. The author cannot be held responsible for personal and/or commercial damages in case of misinterpreting and misunderstanding any part of this Book

Table of Contents

Introduction...6

Red 8

    Apple Citrus Sangria...9

    Berry Bourbon Wine Cocktail 11

    Blackberry Wine Slushie 13

    Bubblegum Sangria..15

    Burgundy & Ginger Fizz 17

    Cabernet Cobbler 19

    Champagne and Wine Cocktail 21

    G&W..23

    New York Sour 25

    Red Devil Margarita 27

Rosé...29

    Basil and White Peach Rosé Crush.................30

    Blushing Mojito 32

    Boozy Berry Frosé 34

Chili-Spiced Watermelon Smash 36

Fruity Coco Punch with Rosé Wine 39

Jasmine & Ginger Kiss 41

Rosé Martini 43

Sherbet Float Punch 45

Spiked Sweet Tea with Fresh Blackberries 47

Sparkling 49

Blackberry and Amaretto Shimmer 50

Champagne Margarita 52

Elderflower Fizz Berry 54

French 75 56

Grapefruit Sangria with Bubbles 58

Ice Blue Frosties 60

1/2 c. Blue Curacao 62

Le Noir Chocolat 63

Pink Blush Bellini 65

Sparkling Sage Lemon Drops 67

The Moonwalk 69

White 71

    Peach Bellini Popsicle Cocktails 72

    Peachy Mint Sangria 74

    Pineapple Scotch Bonnet Mulled Wine Cocktail 76

    Pinot Grigio Sour 78

    Strawberry, Gin, and White Wine Cooler 80

    The Bee's Knees 82

    Vodka Grapelicious 84

    Whatamelon, Wine? 87

    White Peach Sangria 89

    White Wine and Cranberry Slushie 91

Author's Afterthoughts 93

About the Author 94

Introduction

On February 19th the Nation celebrates National Drink Wine Day – not that we need an excuse!

But before we wine down with our 40 best wine cocktail recipes here are some fun facts to share over a glass or two.

- Drinking red wine can have a positive effect on your sex life as it can increase testosterone levels.
- According to the most up to date statistics, Andorra, with a population of just under 70,000 quaffs the most wine, consuming 1,039,781 gallons per year.
- The top 5 USA states for wine consumption are; Washington, New Hampshire, Vermont, Massachusetts and New Jersey.
- Don't hang on to that bottle of Rose; it's not meant to be aged. All Rose wines should be enjoyed within a few years of their release.
- Oenophobia is the name for people who have a morbid fear of wine. Yep, there really are people who are wine phobic!
- Novinophobia, on the other hand, is the fear of running out of wine!
- Upon the signing of the Declaration of Independence, representatives drank a toast with glasses of Madeira.
- The record for the longest flight of a sparkling wine cork is 177 feet and 9 inches.
- Wine is cholesterol and fat-free.
- There is a spa in Japan where you can bathe in sake, Green tea or red wine – don't drink the bathwater!

Red

Apple Citrus Sangria

A zesty, tart apple and citrus sangria is totally refreshing.

Servings: 6-8

Total Time: 6 to 8 Servings

Ingredients:

- 2 Granny Smith apples (cored, cut into ¾" slices)
- Peel of 1 orange
- 2 cinnamon sticks
- ¾ cup brandy
- ½ cup freshly squeezed lemon juice
- ⅓ cup sugar
- ¾ cup freshly squeezed orange juice
- ¼ cup orange liqueur
- Ice
- 1 cup club soda
- 1 (750-ml) bottle Spanish red wine
- Orange slices (to serve)

Directions:

1. In a large jug or pitcher, add the apples together with the orange peel, cinnamon sticks, brandy, freshly squeezed juices, sugar and orange liqueur and stir well to combine totally. Set to one side, at room temperature, for 60 minutes.

2. Pour in the wine, and stir well.

3. Serve in an ice-filled glass, top up with club soda and garnish with orange slices.

Berry Bourbon Wine Cocktail

If you enjoy bourbon, you will love this red wine, berry and bourbon-infused cocktail. It's definitely one for the grown-ups!

Servings: 1

Total Time: 3mins

Ingredients:

- 3 fresh blackberries (rinsed)
- ½ ounce simple syrup
- 1½ ounces red wine
- 1 ounce bourbon
- ½ ounce freshly squeezed lemon juice
- 2 dashes Angostura bitters
- Ice
- Blackberries (to garnish)

Directions:

1. In a cocktail mixer, muddle the blackberries with the simple syrup.

2. Add the red wine, bourbon, lemon juice, and bitters and shake it all about for 10 seconds.

3. Strain, using a fine mesh nylon strainer into an ice-filled cocktail glass.

4. Add a few berries to garnish.

Blackberry Wine Slushie

Slushies aren't just for the little ones. If you need to cool down, or off, try this red wine and vodka slushie!

Servings: 1

Total Time: 3mins

Ingredients:

- 1½ ounces vodka
- 5 fresh blackberries
- 1 ounce freshly squeezed orange juice
- 4 ounces red wine
- 1 tsp agave nectar
- 2 fresh blackberries (to garnish)

Directions:

1. Add the vodka, orange juice, red wine, and agave nectar to an ice-filled blender and shake it all about.

2. Pour the cocktail into a stem-less wine glass.

3. Garnish with blackberries.

Bubblegum Sangria

A fun punch perfect for a get-together or party.

Servings: 8

Total Time: 12hours 7mins

Ingredients:

- ¼ cup gumballs
- 1 cup vodka
- 1 (750ml) bottle red wine
- 1 cup sparkling strawberry watermelon juice
- 1 peach (pitted, sliced)
- 1 orange (pitted, sliced)
- ½ cup fresh raspberries
- Ice

Directions:

1. Add the gumballs to a jar.

2. Pour the vodka over the gumballs. Cover the jar and allow this to rest for no less than 12 hours.

3. Transfer the gumballs and vodka to a large jug or pitcher; add the vodka, red, wine, sparkling watermelon juice, along with the sliced fruits and fresh raspberries.

4. Stir, add ice and enjoy.

Burgundy & Ginger Fizz

A fabulously fruity and fantastically fizzy, red wine cocktail.

Servings: 1

Total Time: 2mins

Ingredients:

- 1 ounce Burgundy wine
- 4 ounces ginger ale
- Ice
- Lemon slice

Directions:

1. Add the wine and ginger ale to a large, ice-filled wine goblet. Stir to combine.

2. Garnish with a lemon slice and serve.

Cabernet Cobbler

A refreshing cabernet sauvignon wine cooler.

Servings: 1

Total Time: 5mins

Ingredients:

- 1 tsp freshly squeezed lemon juice
- 2 ounces soda water (chilled)
- 1 tsp superfine sugar
- Ice
- 4 ounces Cabernet Sauvignon red wine (chilled)
- Orange slice

Directions:

1. Add the lemon juice and soda water to a large wine goblet, add the sugar and stir to dissolve.

2. Add ice to the glass and pour over the red wine.

3. Gently stir.

4. Garnish with a slice of orange and enjoy.

Champagne and Wine Cocktail

Add some pizzazz to your favorite glass of red. All you have to do to make this cocktail sparkle is choose two flavors that are compatible with one another, for instance, a light Champagne pairs well with a fruity, rather than a dry, full-bodied red.

Servings: 1

Total Time: 5mins

Ingredients:

- 2 ounces red wine
- Ice cubes
- 4 ounces Champagne

Directions:

1. Add the red wine to a cocktail shaker filled with half a dozen ice cubes.

2. Add the Champagne to the cocktail shaker.

3. Gently swirl the cocktail shaker to ensure that the red wine and Champagne combines, but be gentle as you don't want the Champagne to get too fizzy.

4. Strain the cocktail into a Champagne flute and serve.

G&W

Forget your usual G&Ts and instead combine gin with red wine for a drink to remember.

Servings: 1

Total Time: 4mins

Ingredients:

- 1½ ounces gin
- 1 ounce Spanish red wine
- ½ ounce simple syrup
- Ice
- ½ ounce freshly squeezed lime juice
- Orange peel (to garnish)

Directions:

1. Add the gin, wine, lime juice, and syrup in a cocktail shaker. Add ice and shake it all about until cold.

2. Strain the cocktail in to a coupe glass and then garnish with a piece of orange peel.

New York Sour

Top a whiskey sour with dry red wine to get an impressive twist on an all-time classic.

Servings: 1

Total Time: 4mins

Ingredients:

- 2 ounces cognac
- ¾ ounce freshly squeezed orange juice
- ¾ ounce freshly squeezed lemon juice
- 2 tsp superfine sugar
- ½ ounce dry red wine

Directions:

1. In an ice-filled cocktail shaker, add the cognac, orange and lemon juices followed by the sugar, and shake it all about for 15 seconds.

2. Strain the cocktail into a chilled Champagne coupe.

3. Carefully and slowly pour in the red wine on the back of a teaspoon resting on top of the liquid; this will help the wine floats on the surface.

4. Enjoy.

Red Devil Margarita

Make a statement with this seriously cool looking layered Margarita.

Servings: 1

Total Time: 6mins

Ingredients:

- 1½ ounces tequila blanco
- ¾ ounce freshly squeezed lime juice freshly
- ¾ ounce simple syrup
- Ice
- Cabernet Sauvignon red wine

Directions:

1. Add the tequila, lime juice and syrup to an ice-filled cocktail shaker.

2. Place a teaspoon, at a 45-degree angle, inside the glass, with the back of the teaspoon facing upwards.

3. Carefully, and slowly pour the red wine over the back of the teaspoon, allowing it to drizzle onto the Margarita.

4. Continue pouring until you have around ¼" of wine in the glass.

Rosé

Basil and White Peach Rosé Crush

The ultimate springtime cocktail, why not watch the sun go down as you sip on this heavenly combination of fresh basil, white peach, gin, and rosé wine.

Servings: 1

Total Time: 5mins

Ingredients:

- 3 leaves fresh basil
- ¼ ounce Aperol
- 1¼ ounces gin
- ¼ ounce freshly squeezed lemon juice
- ¼ ounce white peach puree
- ¼ ounce simple sugar syrup
- Ice
- Splash dry rosé wine

Directions:

1. Add the basil to a cocktail mixer and mash with the end of a wooden spoon. Pour in the Aperol, gin, lemon juice, peach puree, and sugar syrup along with a handful of ice.

2. Shake for 15-20 seconds until chilled then strain into a tall glass filled with ice.

3. Top with the rose wine and serve!

Blushing Mojito

A bright berry and wine twist, on the classic lime and rum mojito is the ultimate summer cocktail.

Servings: 1

Total Time: 7mins

Ingredients:

- 2 fresh strawberries (hulled, diced)
- 2 wedges lime
- 1 tsp agave nectar
- 6 leaves mint
- Crushed ice
- ½ cup rosé wine (well chilled)
- ¼ cup soda water (well chilled)

Directions:

1. Add the strawberries, lime wedges, agave nectar, and mint to a tall glass, muddle, and mash using the end of a wooden spoon.

2. Fill the glass with crushed ice and top with wine, then soda water.

3. Enjoy!

Boozy Berry Frosé

The ultimate slushie for grownups made with strawberry syrup, vodka, and rosé wine. Perfect for girl's night!

Servings: 4

Total Time: 8hours 10mins

Ingredients:

- 1 (750ml) bottle rosé wine
- 5 tbsp strawberry flavor syrup
- ¼ cup good quality vodka
- Ice

Directions:

1. Pour the wine into a large zip lock bag and pop in the freezer overnight (the mixture should still be a little slushy).

2. When ready to serve, add the semi-frozen wine, strawberry syrup, and vodka. Blitz until smooth, if the mixture is too slushy add a little ice and blitz again.

3. Pour into wine glasses and serve!

Chili-Spiced Watermelon Smash

If you're feeling a little adventurous, then you have to try this spicy, sweet concoction, which combines fresh watermelon, Fresno chili, tequila, and rosé wine.

Servings: 1

Total Time: 7mins

Ingredients:

- 1 slice Fresno chili
- 2 chunks fresh watermelon
- ¾ ounce pink grapefruit juice
- 1½ ounces tequila
- ¼ ounce freshly squeezed lime juice
- ½ ounce simple sugar syrup
- Ice
- Crushed ice
- Rosé wine

Directions:

1. Add the Fresno chili and fresh watermelon to a cocktail mixer, mash together using the end of a wooden spoon.

2. Pour in the grapefruit juice, tequila, lime juice, and sugar syrup along with a handful of ice.

3. Shake for 20-25 seconds until well chilled.

4. Strain into a tall glass filled with crushed ice. Top until full with rosé wine, enjoy!

Fruity Coco Punch with Rosé Wine

A fruity part punch with tropical and refreshing coconut water and a generous glug of rosé wine.

Servings: 6

Total Time: 7mins

Ingredients:

- 2 cups rosé wine (well chilled)
- 3 cups pineapple flavored coconut water (well chilled)
- 1 cup freshly squeezed orange juice
- Splash grenadine
- 2 drops pink food gel
- 2½ cups mixed fruit (chopped)
- Ice
- Pineapple wedges

Directions:

1. Add the wine, coconut water, orange juice, grenadine, and pink food gel to a punch bowl. Stir well and toss in the fruit.

2. Chill for 2-3 hours.

3. Serve with ice-filled glasses garnished with a wedge of pineapple.

Jasmine & Ginger Kiss

Impress your friends with a floral and fragrant blend of fresh ginger, jasmine tea, vodka, and rosé wine.

Servings: 4

Total Time: 5mins

Ingredients:

- ⅓ cup simple sugar syrup
- 1½" chunk fresh ginger (peeled, sliced)
- 3 ounces good quality vodka
- 6 ounces freshly brewed jasmine tea (cooled)
- 1½ ounces freshly squeezed lemon juice
- Ice
- Splash rosé wine

Directions:

1. Add the sugar syrup and ginger to a cocktail mixer and mash together using the end of a wooden spoon.

2. Pour in the vodka, jasmine tea, and lemon juice along with a handful of ice. Shake well for 15-20 seconds until chilled.

3. Strain into four coupes and top each until full with rosé wine.

4. Enjoy!

Rosé Martini

Shake up the classic martini and stir it with rosé wine instead of gin for a lighter and more drinkable tipple.

Servings: 1

Total Time: 5mins

Ingredients:

- 1 ounce dry vermouth
- 2 ounces rosé wine (well chilled)
- Ice
- Strawberry (for rim)

Directions:

1. Add the vermouth and wine to an ice-filled cocktail mixer. Shake for 15-20 seconds until chilled.

2. Strain into a martini glass and decorate the rim with a fresh strawberry.

Sherbet Float Punch

A sweet and sour punch spiked with white rum and rosé wine, guaranteed to bring fizz and excitement to any get-together.

Servings: 12

Total Time: 10mins

Ingredients:

- ½ gallon raspberry flavor sherbet
- 2 (750ml) bottles rosé wine (well chilled)
- 4 cups lemon and lime soda (well chilled)
- 1 cup good quality rum

Directions:

1. Scoop half of the raspberry sherbet into a punch bowl.

2. Pour the chilled wine, soda, and rum over the sherbet in the bowl. Scoop the remaining sherbet and float it on top of the punch.

3. Serve straight away.

Spiked Sweet Tea with Fresh Blackberries

Add a splash of bourbon and rosé to your next batch of sweet tea for a deliciously boozy and refreshing tipple. We won't tell!

Servings: 8

Total Time: 3hours 10mins

Ingredients:

- 7 tbsp sugar dissolved in 7 tbsp hot water
- 2 cups blueberries
- 1½ cups rosé wine
- 2 cups freshly brewed black tea (cooled)
- ¾ cup freshly squeezed lemon juice
- 1 cup bourbon whiskey
- 8 slices lemon
- Ice

Directions:

1. Add the sugar water and ¾ of the blueberries to a blender, blitz until smooth. Strain the puree (pressing the mixture to release as much as possible) into a pitcher.

2. Pour in the wine, tea, lemon juice, and whiskey. Stir and chill for 2-3 hours.

3. Slice the remaining blueberries in half and add to the pitcher before serving. Garnish serving glasses with a slice of lemon and fill with ice.

Sparkling

Blackberry and Amaretto Shimmer

Nutty almond liqueur pairs perfectly with dry and floral Italian Prosecco and a handful of tart, juicy berries.

Servings: 1

Total Time: 5mins

Ingredients:

- 1 tbsp amaretto liqueur
- ½ cup Prosecco (well chilled)
- 3-4 fresh blackberries

Directions:

1. Add the amaretto and Prosecco to a flute glass. Gently stir.

2. Toss in a few blackberries and serve!

Champagne Margarita

A classy twist on the classic tequila margarita.

Servings: 1

Total Time: 5mins

Ingredients:

- Wedge of lime (for rim)
- Sea salt (for rim)
- Ice
- 2 ounces fresh lime juice
- 3 ounces white tequila
- ½ tsp orange liqueur
- 1 ounce simple sugar syrup
- Champagne (well chilled)

Directions:

1. Run a wedge of the lime around the rim of a margarita glass. Sprinkle sea salt into a shallow dish and then dip the rim of the glass into it. Fill the glass with ice.

2. Add ice to a cocktail mixer along with the lime juice, orange liqueur, tequila and sugar syrup. Shake well and strain into the glass.

3. Carefully top until full with Champagne and serve!

Elderflower Fizz Berry

Floral, perfumed elderflower, homemade cranberry syrup, and sparkling wine make for an irresistibly sophisticated tipple.

Servings: 1

Total Time: 5mins

Ingredients:

- 1 ounce cranberry flavor syrup
- 1 ounce French elderflower liqueur
- 4 ounces sparkling wine (well chilled)
- 4-6 fresh cranberries
- Granulated sugar

Directions:

1. Pour the cranberry syrup and elderflower liqueur into a flute glass, stir well and top until full with sparkling wine.

2. Spear the cranberries on a toothpick, sprinkle the sugar onto a plate and roll the cranberry skewer in the sugar until the berries are lightly coated. Garnish the cocktail with the sugar-coated cranberry skewer.

French 75

The French 75 is a classic Champagne cocktail first made over 60 years ago and named after the French WWI 75 field gun.

Servings: 1

Total Time: 5mins

Ingredients:

- 1 ounce fresh lemon juice
- 2 ounces gin
- 2 tsp granulated sugar
- Ice
- Champagne (well chilled)
- Lemon twist (for garnish)

Directions:

1. Add the lemon juice, gin, and sugar to an ice-filled cocktail mixer. Shake for 15-20 seconds until cold.

2. Strain into a flute glass and top slowly, until full, with Champagne. Garnish with a lemon twist.

Grapefruit Sangria with Bubbles

A refreshing and fruity up market sangria guaranteed to get the party started!

Servings: 8

Total Time: 8hours 5mins

Ingredients:

- Small handful fresh mint
- ¼ cup simple sugar syrup
- ½ pink grapefruit (peeled, chopped into chunks)
- 1 cup fresh ruby red grapefruit juice
- 1 cup French rosé wine aperitif
- 1 (750ml) bottle Cava (well chilled)
- Ice

Directions:

1. Add the mint leaves and sugar syrup the bottom of a pitcher and muddle with a wooden spoon.

2. Toss in the chunks of pink grapefruit.

3. Pour in the juice, wine aperitif and top with Cava. Stir gently and chill overnight.

4. When ready to serve, add some ice to the pitcher and enjoy!

Ice Blue Frosties

These ice blue, grownup frosties are as pretty as they are delicious!

Servings: 4

Total Time: 7mins

Ingredients:

- ½ cup cloudy lemonade
- 1 cup sparkling wine (well chilled)
- 1 cup good quality vodka
- 3 cups ice
- Wedge lemon
- Blue sanding sugar

Directions:

4. Add the lemonade, sparkling wine, vodka, and ice to a blender. Blitz until combined (you may need to do this in several small goes as the sparkling wine tends to 'froth up').

5. Take 4 short glasses. Run the lemon wedge around the rim of each and then dip in blue sanding sugar.

6. Pour the blended cocktail into the decorated glasses and serve straight away.

1/2 c. Blue Curacao

Le Noir Chocolat

A rich and indulgent twist on the classic Black Velvet cocktail made with dark stout beer and Champagne.

Servings: 1

Total Time: 5mins

Ingredients:

- 4 ounces chocolate flavor stout beer (well chilled)
- Couple dashes orange bitters
- 2 ounces Champagne (well chilled)
- 2" piece fresh orange peel

Directions:

1. Add the chocolate stout beer and orange bitters to a flute glass. Top with Champagne and garnish with a piece of orange peel.

Pink Blush Bellini

The next time you are looking for a fizzy tipple to serve with brunch or breakfast swap the classic peach Bellini for this blush colored berry version made with fresh strawberry puree.

Servings: 1

Total Time: 5mins

Ingredients:

- 1 ounce fresh strawberries (hulled, pureed in a blender)
- 3 ounces Prosecco (well chilled)
- 1 large strawberry (for rim)

Directions:

1. Pour the puree into the base of a flute glass. Slowly top with chilled Prosecco.

2. Decorate the rim with a fresh strawberry and serve.

Sparkling Sage Lemon Drops

Woodsy sage and zesty lemon are a match made in heaven, especially when topped with bubbly Spanish sparkling wine.

Servings: 6

Total Time: 1hours 10mins

Ingredients:

- Sage and Lemon Sugar Syrup:
- 6 ounces water
- 1 cup + 1 tbsp granulated sugar
- 10 sage leaves
- Juice of 2 medium lemons

Cocktail:

- 6 ounces prepared syrup
- 1 (750ml) bottle Spanish Cava (well chilled)
- 6 lemon zest twists
- 6 sage leaves

Directions:

1. Add the water, sugar, sage, and lemon juice in a saucepan over moderately high heat. Bring to a boil then take off the heat and set to one side for an hour.

2. Strain the syrup into a resealable bottle.

3. Pour 1 ounce of syrup into each of 6 flutes glasses Top each until full with Cava and garnish each cocktail with a lemon twist and a sage leaf. Enjoy!

The Moonwalk

This delicious Champagne cocktail was first shaken up at the Savoy Hotel, London to commemorate the legendary American moon landing in 1969. It was also, the first thing that Buzz Aldrin and Neil Armstrong sipped, on returning to planet Earth!

Servings: 1

Total Time: 7mins

Ingredients:

- Few drops rosewater
- 1 ounce orange liqueur
- 1 ounce grapefruit juice
- Ice
- Champagne (well chilled)

Directions:

1. Add the rosewater, orange liqueur, and grapefruit juice to an ice-filled cocktail mixer. Shake for 15-20 seconds.

2. Strain into a flute glass and top until full with Champagne.

3. Enjoy!

White

Peach Bellini Popsicle Cocktails

Adults will love these wine infused popsicles. Pop them in the freezer, and you are good to go!

Servings: 4-8*

Total Time: 4hours 10mins

Ingredients:

- 2 cups peaches (pitted, sliced)
- 1 cup Sauvignon Blanc white wine
- ¼ cup freshly squeezed orange juice
- Popsicle molds
- Wooden sticks

Directions:

1. Add the peaches, wine and orange juice to a food blender and blend until lump free and smooth.

2. Pour the mixture into popsicle molds and transfer to the freezer for 90 minutes.

3. Take out of the freezer and insert a popsicle stick into center of the mold.

4. Transfer to the freezer for 3-4 hours.

5. *Depending on the size of your popsicle mold.

Peachy Mint Sangria

Chardonnay's vanilla and buttery notes blend quite deliciously with peach nectar and orange vodka.

Servings: 4

Total Time: 10mins

Ingredients:

- 30-35 mint leaves
- Ice cubes
- 12 ounces Chardonnay wine
- 12 ounces peach nectar
- 4 ounces orange vodka
- 4 peach slices (to garnish)

Directions:

1. First gently rub the mint leaves between clean palms; this will release their oils.

2. Place the mint in the bottom of a pitcher or jug.

3. Add ice, followed by the Chardonnay, peach nectar, and vodka. Stir to combine.

4. Garnish slices of fresh peach.

Pineapple Scotch Bonnet Mulled Wine Cocktail

This cocktail has fiery heat thanks to the Scotch Bonnet balanced with the fruity sweetness of pineapple and orange juice.

Servings: 4

Total Time: 24hours 10mins

Ingredients:

- ½ fresh pineapple (peeled, cored, roughly chopped)
- ½ cup Chardonnay
- ¼ cup freshly squeezed orange juice
- 1 Scotch Bonnet chile pepper

Directions:

1. Add the pineapple along with the Chardonnay and orange juice to a food blender and process to a puree.

2. Transfer the puree to a large bowl and stir in the Scotch Bonnet.

3. Transfer to the fridge to chill for one day.

4. When you are ready to serve, transfer the mixture to a pan, stir well and warm. Discard the pepper before serving.

Pinot Grigio Sour

Citrus fruit juices and Pinot Grigio are a winning combination; the wine's punchy acidity marries perfectly with orange and lemon juice.

Servings: 2

Total Time: 5mins

Ingredients:

- Ice
- 4 ounces Barefoot Pinot Grigio
- 2 ounces freshly squeezed orange juice
- 1 ounce freshly squeezed lemon juice
- ½ ounce simple syrup
- 2 cherries (to garnish)

Directions:

1. To an ice-filled cocktail shaker add the wine, orange juice, lemon juice, and syrup.

2. Shake it all about.

3. Strain the cocktail into two, ice-filled rocks glasses.

4. Garnish each glass with a cherry and enjoy.

Strawberry, Gin, and White Wine Cooler

Pinos Gris, not to be confused with Pinot Grigot is a full-bodied, rich, and spicy wine and is currently gaining in popularity.

Servings: 1

Total Time: 4mins

Ingredients:

- 3 fresh strawberries (hulled, chopped)
- Juice of ¼ fresh lemon
- 3 ounces Pinot Gris
- Agave nectar (to taste)
- 1 ounce gin
- Ice
- 1 slice strawberry (to garnish)

Directions:

1. In a cocktail shaker muddle the strawberries, lemon juice, wine and, to taste, the agave nectar.

2. Add the gin along with some ice and shake well.

3. Strain the cocktail in to an ice-filled wine glass and then garnish with a slice of strawberry.

The Bee's Knees

With honey, fresh lemon, and sweet Moscato wine this cocktail really is the Bee's Knees!

Servings: 1

Total Time: 3mins

Ingredients:

- 1½ tbsp raw honey
- ½ tbsp hot water
- 4 ounces Moscato white wine (well chilled)
- 2½ tsp freshly squeezed lemon juice
- Crushed ice
- Slice lemon

Directions:

1. In a glass, dissolve the honey in hot water. Pour in the Moscato and lemon juice. Stir well and carefully fill the glass with crushed ice.

2. Decorate with a slice of lemon.

3. Serve straight away!

Vodka Grapelicious

Chardonnay, Processo and fresh grapes come together in this vodka, wine cocktail.

Servings: 1

Total Time: 15mins

Ingredients:

- ½ ounce simple syrup
- 5 seedless grapes
- 2 mint sprigs
- 1¼ ounces vanilla vodka
- ½ ounce freshly squeezed lemon juice
- 1 ounce Chardonnay
- Ice
- Prosecco (chilled)
- 2 grapes (to garnish)

Directions:

1. First, make the syrup by combining equal parts of hot water with sugar and stir until totally dissolved. Allow to cool.

2. Add the grapes, mint, and prepared syrup to a cocktail shaker and muddle.

3. Add the vodka and follow by the freshly squeezed lemon juice, Chardonnay, and ice.

4. Shake it all about.

5. Strain the cocktail into a glass and top with chilled Prosecco.

6. Garnish with a couple of grapes and enjoy.

Whatamelon, Wine?

Wine and vodka are two great tastes that pair well together, and Sauvignon Blanc's refreshing flavor is perfect with watermelon juice and zesty lemon.

Servings: 1

Total Time: 45mins

Ingredients:

- 1 ounce Sauvignon Blanc
- 1 ounce vodka
- 1 ounce watermelon juice
- 1 ounce of simple syrup
- ½ ounce lemon
- Ice
- 1½ ounce soda water

Directions:

1. Make the simple syrup by mixing equal parts of sugar and hot water until the sugar totally dissolves. Allow to cool.

2. Add the wine, vodka, prepared syrup and lemon to an ice-filled cocktail shaker and shake it all about,

3. Strain in to an ice-filled glass and top with the soda water.

White Peach Sangria

The perfect party punch for any occasion.

Servings: 10

Total Time: 15mins

Ingredients:

- 1 bottle Pinot Grigio
- 1¼ cups mango rum
- 1¼ cups white peach schnapps
- 12 squeezes fresh lemon
- 12 squeezes fresh lime
- 12 squeezes fresh orange
- 2½ cups lemon-lime soda
- Ice

Directions:

1. Combine the wine, followed by the rum, schnapps, fresh lemon juice, lime juice, orange juice and lemon-lime soda in a punch bowl, filled three-quarters of the way full of ice.

2. Stir to combine.

3. Serve.

White Wine and Cranberry Slushie

White wine slushies, made with cranberry juice and limeade are irresistible.

Servings: 6

Total Time: 10mins

Ingredients:

- 1 (750ml) bottle of New Zealand Sauvignon Blanc
- 1 (12 ounce) can limeade concentrate (frozen)
- 1 cup cranberry juice

Directions:

1. Add the wine, limeade and cranberry juice to a blender and process until smooth. If the mixture is too liquid or too warm, transfer to the freezer, stirring every half an hour until a perfect slushy texture forms.

Author's Afterthoughts

Thanks ever so much to each of my cherished readers for investing the time to read this book!

I know you could have picked from many other books but you chose this one. So a big thanks for downloading this book and reading all the way to the end.

If you enjoyed this book or received value from it, I'd like to ask you for a favor. Please take a few minutes to post an honest and heartfelt review on Amazon.com. Your support does make a difference and helps to benefit other people.

Thanks!

Daniel Humphreys

About the Author

Daniel Humphreys

Many people will ask me if I am German or Norman, and my answer is that I am 100% unique! Joking aside, I owe my cooking influence mainly to my mother who was British! I can certainly make a mean Sheppard's pie, but when it comes to preparing Bratwurst sausages and drinking beer with friends, I am also all in!

I am taking you on this culinary journey with me and hope you can appreciate my diversified background. In my 15 years career as a chef, I never had a dish returned to me by one of clients, so that should say something about me! Actually, I will take that back. My worst critic is my four years old son, who refuses to taste anything that is green color. That shall pass, I am sure.

My hope is to help my children discover the joy of cooking and sharing their creations with their loved ones, like I did all my life. When you develop a passion for cooking and my suspicious is that you have one as well, it usually sticks for life. The best advice I can give anyone as a professional chef is invest. Invest your time, your heart in each meal you are creating. Invest also a little money in good cooking hardware and quality ingredients. But most of all enjoy every meal you prepare with YOUR friends and family!

Made in the USA
Coppell, TX
13 December 2023

26062497R00059